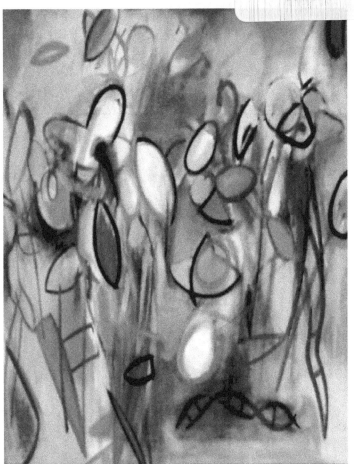

All About Living

by Molly Brogan

Published By Molly Brogan Enterprises: Detroit, MI

Copyright © 2010 by Molly Brogan

ISBN 978 0 557 26574 9

Cover Art by Vivian George

Printed in the United States of America

DEDICATION

For the past few years, I have had the privilege of joining dialogues with people from all over the globe, on the internet, over the telephone and in person. These conversations were not only about my books, but also about life in general. I have gained a fresh depth of understanding about the world's different individual and collective cultures, traditions, historical perspectives and viewpoints. New friends and kindred spirits are discovered and developed through these discussions. Plato's idea that dialogue raises consciousness has been demonstrated to me in the most exquisite way, as I apply what I learn to my life and writing. I feel infinite gratitude for all the groups and individuals that continue to contribute to these dialogues.

The wonderment of observing the emergence of a global society is not lost on me. Our technology truly is an extension of who we are as it allows us to connect with other people and cultures around the planet in internet groups, instant messaging, twitters and video conferences. As events occur, whether an act of terrorism or the award of the Nobel Prize, we discuss them, each participant offering a different viewpoint and knowledge base. The immediacy of information through computer search engines allows us all to keep up and expand our own horizons while communing through words. Computer translators that instantly transform pages of words allow those of us that speak different languages to effortlessly understand each other. This age of humanity truly supports the depth and breadth of our relationships, and simultaneously provides these same tools for examination of self.

While discussing the topics of God, evil, forgiveness and shadow, among others included in this book, I witness my own ideas taking shape as I express them. After considerable encouragement from readers and friends to publish some of my ideas as I share them in these dialogues, I remembered one of my favorite books *The World As I See It* by Albert Einstein. In the original edition of this book (1934) Einstein compiled speeches and letters concerning his ideas on spirituality. As years went by, his publishers compiled other editions for him under the same title, with what they felt were relevant topics for Einstein opinion. It seemed to me that this format, devoting chapters to topics on common human relevance, would be the best arrangement for my own series, which I have entitled *All About Living*. In these books, I will be including my ideas that I examine with readers and friends about life and living. I hope you enjoy *Book 1* of *All About Living*, as well as the subsequent books that will follow.

I dedicate these books to everyone who has
contributed to these dialogues and participated in
these exchanges. Many thanks and God bless.

Molly Brogan

TABLE OF CONTENTS

I see you

And feel you

And think

We are

All about living

Until I am swept away

Beyond the you

And the me

Into the meaning of us

Where words

Are not necessary

And there is

Only love.

AGE OF ETHICS

EXTENDING US AT ONCE INTERNALLY AND EXTERNALLY, TECHNOLOGY USHERS US INTO THE AGE OF ETHICS

The transition into the age of ethics has just begun and will take decades to emerge. It will be, I think, a fascinating transition. Our notions of trust will, out of necessity, become central and evolve. The transition from the information age to the age of ethics is a dynamic dialectic. Trusting ourselves to know that despite our fallibilities and mistakes, we will persevere and grow is essential.

Just as the personal computer ushered us into the age of information, the personal communication device will usher us into the age of ethics. With communications technology developing at an accelerated rate, there is little happening in the world that can be hidden anymore. Sure, there are areas of the world that are underdeveloped, without technology and operating at the bottom of Maslow's hierarchy. Yet, as this is the age of global experience, they will be carried along. Could this be part of life's grand design as well? Can we trust that it is?

Transparency will be fundamental to the age of ethics. Because any conversation or event can be exposed by recording it with a cell phone and posting it on the internet, or sending it to a television station, we will begin to behave in ways that are necessarily ethical. As more human rights indignities are exposed, they will also fall away, as global economies emerge and regional or national economies find it difficult to operate in isolation.

Will thought follow action? Undoubtedly. As we act in ethical ways, our thought patterns will develop in those ways also - until we realize through the position of the witness – until we can observe that our external structures need not dictate our internal structures. Then, we are free of even those limits. The moral question: "What would I do if everyone were watching me?" will become central, yet still externally driven. But it will lead to the understanding that I am everyone else, which is internally driven, and will naturally create action based on the greater good.

I think that for many of us, the age of ethics will not depend on external technology. It will come about with internal awakening. What the philosopher Rudolph Steiner would call ethical individualism will occur as we begin to feel our connection to all life, with the life current flowing through us to be reflected back in our experience in everything we see. When we are in harmony with life in this way, a natural ethic will emerge, and be integral to our every expression. We will be living more intuitively, and respond to our feeling of harmony in our bodies, minds and souls.

Sometimes, what we notice first in our experience, is the old falling away with deconstruction. What comes into being to fill the space is not as apparent. Some will try to hold fast to what is falling away, and cries of naïveté or conspiracy will come from those that focus on barriers to entry and current problems. If we focus on the problem, it will remain the experience. If we focus on the solution, the problem will fall away with deconstruction, and the solution will emerge. If we focus on the vision, and live as if it is the current paradigm, the world transforms, offering much more than a single solution. The next paradigm allows for our intuition, ethics, spirituality, creativity, connectedness, unity and brilliance. Jumping the curve to the next paradigm is bold. Let's be bold!

We all have belief; it is a basic component of human psychology – seen in the individual conscious and subconscious minds. Beyond the individual, belief is manifest socially. This social or group form of belief is seen in religious congregations, or along the lines of communities agreeing on ethical behavior. Belief in social agreements (such as stopping at the stop lights, not bumping those in front of us in line at the register with shopping carts, returning our library books, not shooting the people that walk down our streets) add structure to life. More severe infractions of the social agreements require laws and enforcement of them.

There are many of us that find no purpose in organized religion. Many do. And many do and don't in different periods of our lives. Such is life. We choose our beliefs and groups to express them, that is, until the One and the many in us, express in unity. At this point, our ethics and actions are one in the same, expressed naturally in our experience, in the flow of creation.

An awareness of how our viewpoint creates our experience naturally allows for an intrinsic morality – one that comes from the inside and moves out, instead of being developed and then imposed from the outside in. We no longer recognize it externally as a social imperative dictating our actions accordingly, but move through it in our experience because our viewpoint allows our connection with all of humanity to provide the basis for moral and ethical behavior.

B EING

OUR BEING NATURALLY INCLUDES OUR PHYSICAL, EMOTIONAL AND MENTAL ASPECTS IN CONSCIOUSNESS

I think that our "being" covers every aspect of who we are, including the trendy "who we really are." Essential being - that part of us that is infinite, that holds our absolute truths, grounds us to the universe, is our awareness, moves the Logos - is just as important as finite and changeable aspects, such as our cellular components, ego, sacral, or consciousness. It is like saying that our rectum is a lesser part of our being because we don't like to think of its function or what passes through. We wipe and flush without a second thought. And yet, when it does not function - it overpowers our awareness, doesn't it? Why - because it too, is valuable to our being and calls for integration. If we honor all aspects of ourselves as equally important, as integrated, they will not feel the need to roar to us.

Even when our body, mind, and spirit are working in integration, we continue to change. Each change in viewpoint brings about a change in individual being and experience. The biographical movie of the life of the singer, songwriter Bob Dylan, *I'm Not There,* has a terrific cast, Heath Ledger, Cate Blanchette, Christian Bale, Richard Gere... each playing a different aspect of Dylan's character as he reinvents himself at different parts of his life by changing his viewpoint and relationship to life. I know that I have done this as I have been called into service of the greater whole by experience to become student, drifter, teacher, wife, mother, activist, prevention specialist, social designer, corporate executive, writer...still, and through each, (each seemed to have their own unique identity,) I felt the heartbeat of the same essential being - the being expressed as me.

In the movie about Dylan, there was an element of suffering for him as he transitioned from persona to persona. This may lend itself to the idea of the lifting of the veil layers during the dark night of the soul, as the ego dies to be reborn. If we can learn to let go of these ego aspects with joy, (can we feel pain while experiencing joy - as in childbirth?) the suffering is unnecessary.

The art of being may just be recognizing finite aspects of being while creating experience in harmony with the infinite aspects of soul and spirit.

If we have the wisdom to see it, our experience presents us with opportunity for the possibility of becoming, and leads us to our own infinite nature if we do not resist. What parts of us are finite and which infinite can be presented in a clash of light and shadow, or in the whisper of the cool wind on our face. Recognition tells us which is which. If seen from the non dual viewpoint, there is no division between.

My experience is that I am all others, which would bring the finite back to the infinite. My feeling is that I am (and we are) in all time, and within this ultimate paradox lies the stillness - no more questions or answers. But then again, what would we talk about? So, the exploration there and back again creates relationship and is sublime.

I know that I reached a point in my journey, where everything was turned inside out. The Essene Seven Mirrors of Relationship is a pretty good idea about the nature of relationships and how to recognize spirit in them. After exploring this idea,

I saw everything differently, and lost my charge on most things that before bothered me. There no longer seemed to be a need to be angry, fearful etc. This was because I stopped looking at what others were "doing" and looked instead at the relationship of the experience to me - what was the message? Because I am all others, what is this experience telling me? What was it telling me about myself, about spirit?

Divine Will is the integral and active aspect of our being. Most religions recognize a power greater than us. Consider, for a moment, the God in us as the source of all creation. Then we would create our reality not by what we DO, but by what we recognize, respect or allow as divine will moves through us. Divine will, then, is our active awareness of the God in us.

If we can position ourselves to live life like this, The Seven Mirrors in the Essene Mystery of Relationship come into play:

Essene Mirrors of Relationship

1. who we are in the moment

2. what we judge in the moment

3. what has been lost, given away or taken away

4. our forgotten love

5. our relationship with God

6. our dark night of the soul

7. our perfection

All of our experience is reflecting to us one, or a combination of these aspects. Author Gregg Braden presents the most comprehensive presentation of these mirrors that I have seen, in his book, *Walking Between the Worlds: The Science of Compassion*. According to this belief, our experience becomes a vibrational mirror that reflects one or some combination of mirrored patterns in our relationship to others. Recognizing the wisdom of the mirror accelerates our evolution of emotion and understanding. The God in us speaks and guides us through the universal law of vibration and our experience unfolds according to divine will.

Some people see the rational viewpoint - reality is what is external to us, measurable and provable - as "the illusion" of reality. My change of viewpoint by including the Mirrors of Relationship transformed everything for me. From that point, I understood that my experience and I are one. I can understand why someone would see the past viewpoint as illusion because it is such a big leap, a complete transformation – a resurrection. To me the word "illusion" has a diminishing connotation to it, as if the prior viewpoint were somehow less. I don't believe that this is the case at all. I think that every state and stage of our being has ultimate value, and is the foundation for the next, like nesting holograms. No part of our experience is less than another. What is rational in us is included in what is trans-rational in us. All is an expression of the God within us. All is awareness of possibility.

The paradox of the one and the many is always an interesting "one." We are all part of the same One. And all of our parts are one - who we are. When all of this is a conscious part of our experience, we have integrated. All parts communicating as one to the single, peaceful moment. And while all of the busy, vast activity of the universe is of us and within us, if we find our peace of mind, there is quiet and serenity. In this peace, we can interact with our experience as we are called to do. Perfection.

I do agree that there is a state of pure being, beyond words and thought and feeling. But I think that we can live in all states at once, each with its own value and expression. In integration, all states can express spirit. All states being and becoming. My ideas and your ideas are expressions of spirit. They cannot be bought or sold, stolen or even hidden. They are, just as we are. But the communion that we feel in the exchange can often uplift us (or not.) Being in relationship is our sacred expression of the one in many. It is our gift of love.

I am convinced that what it means to be a human "being" is ultimately non local, inclusive of all time, and the awareness of experience (as well as the creator.) The rest is just stories that project on the screen of our experience, lit with the divine light of the life within us. Commitment to that life, confidence in the witness, and love expressed from the one to the many and back again are the mechanics of our projector that give form to possibility.

Rationality is a function of mind that allows order in our experience with questions and answers, cause and effect, problems and solutions. This is important because it leads us to greater awareness. It is also limiting because it traps us in the mind if we can go no farther. What is farther is enormous human potentiality that is transrational - that includes the rational yet is more, because it is not dependent on the duality of cause and effect, me - not me, changeability, psychology or recognition of locality in experience. Yogis spend lifetimes perfecting the transrational experience of the human being, yet eventually this also becomes limiting because it is conditional to method. The awareness of self which ultimately includes all others and the world, is, it seems to me, the simple means of my being. But I am young, and may not be seeing the whole picture yet.

CHANGE

WHERE THERE IS A DISTICTION BETWEEN LIFE AND DEATH, THERE IS CHANGE

Change happens. It is part of the human experience. It can be a wonderful gift, if we understand the process. There is a great deal of information available about skills for managing change. But the most important skills that we can master are the ones that give us an understanding of ourselves, and how we, ourselves, facilitate change in our lives.

Our capacity for paradox is probably the most important factor in our ability to change. When we are presented with a paradox, or two ideas that seem to be opposing, do we choose one, or take a step back and look for a way that they can complement each other? In every paradox, what seems to be opposing can be seen as complimentary and in fact, part of a larger spectrum, from a wider viewpoint. To do this, we must be the proverbial raftsman on the river who maintains his balance, not despite the river or because of the river but with the river. We become the paradox. Usually, this is done, not by action, but by a change in viewpoint. We recognize the relationships between the two rather than choosing between the two. We reconcile what seem to be opposites by seeing the larger picture and owning it.

Determining the spectral nature of paradox might require an ability to develop and sustain relationship. If the change you are experiencing affects not only you but also a larger group, your understanding of the nature of relationship may be the key to successful change. Bringing a group to a wider perspective will take a peaceful resolve and understanding of the nature of group dynamics. Trust, if not previously established, must be inherent in the group. This will take time, communication, and allowance of the natural flow of energy within the group. The real question here becomes, what is my relationship to other? What are they reflecting to me about self and change? In the moment, what comes up will tell you which, if any, action is needed. A strong group network and a clear understanding of your relationship with it and its members will allow trust and help sustain peace in the midst of tension.

Another critical element of change is anamnesis, or the remembrance of our own essential being, that part of us that we bring to manifestation, our own spirit. If we are centered here during the experience of change, all that is presented to us is accepted and allowed as a reflection of spirit. Every time we move into change, there is a process of reaching within and tapping into faith and agency that allows transformation or at least, transition. Our call to action is an internal call. Our trust is rooted in the deepest parts of ourselves and extends outwards, becoming infectious and affirming. Change is sustained only with a change in our own viewpoint, and this often includes the recognition of a greater, common, viewpoint. This change in viewpoint is the crèche of experience manifest. This is essential change.

DECONSTRUCTION

IT MAY FEEL CHAOTIC, BUT DECONSTURCTION REMOVES LIMITATION MAKING SPACE FOR POSSIBILITY

Sometimes, when things seem to be falling apart in our lives, it is happening to allow us to move on in ways that we would not otherwise, because we would hold on to what we have now. Our will is to keep something the same, divine will is to allow change. What we don't see is that the change is wonderful and so we get wrapped up in the bad feeling that things are falling apart. Resist not! It isn't easy to enjoy deconstruction. But when it starts happening to me, I have begun to notice it now, and I can have faith that something wonderful is about to occur in my life.

Deconstruction is a difficult process for all of us. As we create, we are reaching within to experience

God and feel our oneness with God and all his glory. As we deconstruct, we are bringing the energy of God back to the world, and making room for divine will in our experience (the deconstruction.) When we have fully embraced both processes, creation and deconstruction occur simultaneously. As we reach within and connect to all creation, we express creation as divine will, making our experience "more" than ever before, adding the possibility that is ours in the moment. This is the crux of coherent integration. There is joy in feeling the connection and honoring the individuation.

Throughout our lives, people will come and go and always reflect aspects of the divine for us. If we have the wisdom to understand and appreciate this, it is easier to allow them their role in divine will and glory in their own life. It is not that we disregard them without caring when they go. It is that we respect the fulfillment of their soul's purpose in this life and the gifts that they have given us.

It is important to have the wisdom to recognize that the deconstruction, or the falling away of the what no longer serves us (death), allows for the new possibility that you bring as you co-create your experience through divine will (life). This recognition is difficult when experiencing the loss of a loved one. Honoring the life of deceased loved ones, and all the wonderful aspects of life that they will continue to hold for you in your heart, can ease your sorrow. What part of yourself did they represent for you? What did their leaving show you? These are the sacred gifts that their lives offer you. These gifts are true blessings. As you find your peace with this, they will find theirs too.

I very often have difficulty embracing deconstruction because what is falling away still gives me comfort and enjoyment. Sometimes, not even that, but it is a known, and I have yet to rationally know what will be taking its place. When this happens, I have to quiet myself and listen deeply to what my heart has to say. Your heart knows what possibility is coming for you. Your free will has chosen it at the soul level. Your intuition is very sharp. Listen to it. It may reveal just a feeling of excitement or self worth, but it will always give you enough to move ahead on faith.

Celebrate creation while feeling gratitude for the deconstruction. Look at patterns that unify in your experience, instead of what is falling apart through division. In the recognition of what is emerging (with spirit) in our experience, we embrace change and honor life. This is what it means to be divine. Look carefully for that thread that links it all together – our relationships and dreams as well as what is on the news, the events around us and information coming to you. There is a golden thread of spirit that is inside each of us and runs through the world. If we can see this thread, we can witness what is being born into the world. We will see patterns of relationships are forming and how the divine spark flows through these relationships, even in the midst of deconstruction. This thread is an ever-present awareness, which is eternal, which is us, that is life.

EVIL

THE FEELING THAT WE ARE IN THE PRESENCE OF EVIL IS OUR INVITATION INTO HEAVEN ON EARTH

There is a wide variety of opinion on the existence of evil. Some see any opposing force as evil, while others think that to be termed evil requires an act resulting in an injury to life of some kind. What are your thoughts? How does your belief about evil affect your life?

The 19th century Christian mystic Thomas Troward defined evil this way: "This is the old original sin of Eve. It is the belief in Evil as a substantive self-originating power. We believe ourselves under the control of all sorts of evils having their climax in Death; but whence does the evil get its power? Not from God, for no diminution of Life can come from the Fountain of

Life…however, evil may have relative existence, it can have no substantive existence of its own. It is not a Living Originating Power. God, the Good, alone is that…What we recognize as Evil is the One Good Power working as Disintegrating Force, because we have not yet learnt to direct it in such a way that it shall perform the functions of transition to higher degrees of Life without any disintegration of our individuality either in person or circumstances. It is this disintegrating action that makes the ONE Power appear evil relatively to ourselves; and, so long as we conceive ourselves thus related to it, it does look as though it were Zero balancing in itself the two opposing forces."

The trick here is to have faith, that what seems to be evil or destructive is simply an object or occurrence that does not meet our value of "good," and so, must be evil. If we can step back, and instead of seeing only two, good and evil, see the spectrum of good, evil and everything in between, we will understand that it is all just myriad of many moving back to the one. It is all part of who we are. Seeing it all in relationship and without specific value, but infinite value, is observing the problem of evil from a non dual viewpoint. Accepting this can be a challenge. It will also be a giant leap in awareness for anyone who can honestly accept all misdeeds and misfortunes, and truly forgive. Part of this too, is the awareness of no separation between self and other, so that all good, and all evil, and all of everything, is who we are. This is the leap from duality to the non dual viewpoint. Because it is a process of compassion and forgiveness, it is often considered to be the leap to Christ consciousness. I don't think that this means that a dualistic viewpoint is less valuable. Dualism has its own value because it allows its own state of consciousness and stage in development. And I don't think that it means that what is considered evil does not exist. But it does change the value that we place on it.

Rudolph Steiner had a wonderful notion of the important "reconciling opposition" that speaks to the internal process of allowing for the recognition of good and evil to bring us to Christ consciousness. Christ redeemed evil with his message of unconditional forgiveness and love, allowing others to join ranks and follow his path. "Do onto others as you would have them do onto you" is an act of accepting the Oneness and individuality inherent in each moment, with compassion.

I think that "evil" is much like fear. Overcoming fear doesn't mean that I will never experience it again in my life. It means that I understand it differently and process it differently than I once did. Overcoming evil is much the same. Once we understand that evil is a value judgment of negativity in our world, and that judgments assigning positive and negative value are a function of mind, but we are much more than our minds, we can transcend our dualistic mental constructs. When seen at this viewpoint, the world is in balance; what we value as good and evil can be seen differently, as aspects of the same experience.

The "knowledge" of the tree of good and evil only begins with the tree, and the first two dimensions for a linear thought. One point up, one down, and the line between gives the thought two dimensions. Add depth, and we can apply up and down, or good and evil, to every level of life from subatomic to cosmic - three dimensional thinking. Add the fourth dimension of time, and we can experience change over time. This gives our thinking changeability. Some would say the fifth dimension to add is compassion - where Christ meets Buddha - and the good and evil become so multi dimensional and non dual that the charge to it changes. Scientists tell us that there are an infinite number of dimensions and each dimension itself is infinite. Somewhere in that process of including dimension to thinking, we must connect with all there is and the God within us. This allows us to transcend duality of the first four dimensions, what is changeable and finite, and sustain awareness the infinite aspects of life.

We sometimes take identity in holding ourselves separate from others as we judge and value the differences. Not good or bad, it is something we humans do as we identify ourselves. This is a function of our ego, which is limited to duality because it creates our identity separate from the world. Here, good and sometimes evil is established as we explore the "I am not" of I AM. This exploration is important to raising consciousness and expanding awareness. Trouble is, the paradox of the Pharisee comes into play in the subtle levels, and what we are so certain we are not, we become, in our entrenched separation.

Luke 18:11- 14   "The Pharisee stood and prayed thus with himself, God, I thank thee, that I am not as other men are, extortioners, unjust, adulterers, or even as this publican. I fast twice in the week; I give tithes of all that I possess. And the publican, standing afar off, would not lift up so much as his eyes unto heaven, but smote upon his breast, saying, God be merciful to me a sinner. I tell you, this man went down to his house justified rather than the other: for every one that exalteth himself shall be abased; and he that humbleth himself shall be exalted."

In other words, if I say I do not want to be like the other man, then I am just like him. To consider the negative aspects of life is to give them life. To engage in or even discuss hatred, brings more hatred. I become what I say I am not, because to say so holds us in separation. By knowing that I AM all, and that which is seen at all otherwise is a "sin," releases us from this paradox. We transcend the exploration of "I am not," our ego and our identity. Our humility leads us into unity, and the unity consciousness allows us into the non dual viewpoint, allows us to "resist not evil", and exempts us from all but our highest potential.

It is a huge leap to accept all the good and the evil, both as integral to life, and as the polarity that allows change in time and space - our separate nature. After all, we are the many and the one. But if we can we see, that while evil exists, it no longer has a negative value, evil becomes the way of yin and yang and balance. If seen with this viewpoint, the balance can bring love and joy. Here, evil is removed from our direct experience. It remains on the outskirts of our consciousness, in the spectrum of human experience, but directly, we are protected because we are not holding it in our thoughts and feelings and no longer give it value.

When we think "bad" things happen in our lives brought on by "evil" doers, we ourselves are assigning those values and blame, and hold ourselves separate, saying "that is evil, I am not that." By doing so, we ourselves bring more of that into our direct experience. When Shiva makes an entrance into the lives of non dual thinkers, no value is assigned to the deconstruction of the event. It is seen in much the Buddhist way, as a natural cycle of events and often taken on faith that construction and creation follow the destruction. What was before a "bad" event brought on by the evil people around me, becomes the dawn of possibility, as Shiva's mighty sword clears the way for it. Non dual thinkers have long gotten over the "woe is me" state of mind when difficulties arise, and instead open themselves to possibility in a quiet state of active anticipation while feeling the connection to everyone and all that is.

I believe that nothing passes through our consciousness without our consent. This means, that at some level within us, and it may be subconscious, conditions are created that invite and allow us to move though our connection, separation, connection process, until it is no longer necessary and we achieve what has been best described as Is-ness. Now, karma may be a filter through which these events are forming. But at the level of Is-ness, or spirit, or God, or pure energy, or whatever you wish to call "it" all, there is only one cause, and that is spirit. There are many levels of cause and effect, including rational, that allow us to reasonably understand the events in our lives. These levels of cause and effect are dualistic, and include our values of good and evil. And, according to where we are in our process, they are all true. But they are the filters that ultimately lead us back to spirit, or keep us stuck somewhere, usually in rationality.

Karma is said to have a powerful pull in terms of cause and effect - it pulls us into repetition or atonement of previous expressions of identity. Much like the ego is the cause effecting personality, karma the cause creating the soul effect. This occurs so that the effect can lure us into introspection of the cause. There is a point in the exploration of karma, that one realizes their own "innate" connection to everyone and all that is, and the karmic patterns that are designed to lead us to this realization. At this point, fear, judgment, polarity, good and evil, cause and effect all fall away because the one and the many in us is realized. If we can take this understanding back into our lives and begin living from it, we are no longer bound to the law of karmic cause and effect, but simply live the "I AM" of everything and all that is in a non dual way.

Here, there can be no intrusion, because there is no separation from one to the other. Who we are and what is possible is reflected to us in the moment. We can live these moments in a separate string, or in the eternal moment or both - the one and the many. However we choose to live these moments, they are a reflection that invites us into spirit and the possibility of more, all ways.

FEAR

GUARDING THE THRESHOLD TO OUR POTENTIALITY FEAR CONSUMES OUR ASPECTS AS WE INSIST ON IT

You need only watch the evening news to see how fear driven humanity has become. So much of what the media presents displays and exacerbates our fears that we have to wonder, how much of our daily individual experience includes fear? Do we need fear? Can we live without it?

Many of the world's finest minds have chimed in about fear. Heidegger brought these fears to the center of his existential philosophy. He argued that the basic anxiety of [humanity] is anxiety about being, as well as anxiety of being-in-the-world. That is, both fear of death and fear of life, of experience and individuation.

Marcus Aurelius thought that if you are distressed by anything external, the pain is not due to the thing itself, but to your estimate of it; and this you have the power to revoke at any moment.

In his inaugural address that was given in the middle of a financial panic in the United States, President Roosevelt taught us "we have nothing but fear is fear itself." This concept set the tone for his administration and the country.

The Buddhists think that mindful meditation relieves us of our fears. Some consider fear to be paradoxical: Fear is what keeps our boundaries. If we do not listen to that fear, that knowledge that there is something imminent that is not us, we will face the second type of fear, the fear that destroys all boundaries.

I think that the feeling of fear is simply a signal. I've found, that when fear comes into my heart or mind, it is my signal to recognize the feeling and all it involves and expand my awareness - feel my connection to all that is and the unity therein. We feel fear in separation, and it's our opportunity to recognize the separation and the oneness together. Is fear part of the human experience? Yes. Must we live in fear? NO.

From my experience, I can tell you that the longer I treat fear as a signal to feel my total connection to life, and have faith that what will happen next will be in accordance with my highest potential, the less fear I experience. Things that triggered fear 5 years ago do not now. By not allowing the feeling to become emotion, (feeling becomes emotion by including memories of other fearful experiences or dread of future difficulties,) the fear is quelled. What comes up more and more now instead of fear is a mild interest, sometimes amusement, but always faith that what is occurring is reflecting to me what I need to recognize in the moment.

I think that there are many, many feelings to feel other than fear. Can we look at starving people and feel compassion? Can we look at that which we judge to be selfish and unworthy of our experience, and see people on the road to awakening... and feel compassion? Then love would be the antidote to fear, I suppose. Fear is easy. We feel it as children and hang on to it because it is "known" and fear of the unknown is worse than fear of the known.

In the US, as generations go on, so does the fear based attitude of racism, but the targeted race changes. During my grandparent's time, the Irish were targets. Now, because Islam (which is irrationally associated with terrorism) is not really a race, but a religion, anyone with medium dark skin is a target, which could be Eastern European,

Indian, Middle Eastern parts of the globe and include, in truth, several different races and religions of people that have a particular physical "look." It is the tendency of our ego to identify with groups, and feel ourselves against others and other groups, that defines our racism in significant but irrational ways. This behavior is fear based.

A relatively innocuous but fear driven statement against one person and for someone else will interrupt cohesion in the group. In terms of self, moving against is always looking away from self. It is human nature none the less. Wrap that up with a big coat of fear - fear of the future, fear of war, fear of attack, fear of economic disaster, fear that I won't be able to keep my stuff or have more stuff or hang on to my irrational fear and anger that allows me to feel in the absence of love, well, you are perfect fodder for herd mentality and those who prey on it. This herd mentality is simply a reflection of changing humanity. It may be that what we are witnessing in this is really the death throes of racism in a global society, as clear lines between groups blur.

It is not possible to find harmony in our lives when it is filled with fear. Sometimes letting go of fear is as easy as taking a deep breath, and finding our faith or compassion in the moment. Sometimes it is as difficult as a dark night of the soul, where we face our fear by understanding that what we fear is a part of us, and accepting the divinity of all that we are by letting go of every "thing" in our experience.

The emotion of fear needs to be recognized and released, so that we can feel our harmony. Life with an unattached and fearless viewpoint allows us to live in tune with the infinite.

FORGIVENESS

EXERCISING FORGIVENESS UNCONDITIONALLY LEADS TO THE AWARENESS OF ONENESS

There seem to be many faces to the process of "forgiveness" being worn these days. Many books, lectures and workshops are available to help us contemplate and adopt forgiving behaviors. We are all taught as children that forgiveness of friends and family is an important part of social life.

The poet William Blake tells us: "In heaven, the only art of living is forgetting and forgiving." This leads us to the notion that forgiveness is key to finding heaven on earth.

The process that the 20th century mystic Neville Goddard presents as forgiveness, takes us beyond separation and cause, and requires that we simply see everyone in their highest potential: "What we mean by forgiveness the identification of the other that we would forgive with the ideal that other wants to embody in the world. And so we do to him what we expect or would like the world to do to us. So whatever I myself would like to embody that is the vision that I must hold of every man that I meet in my world; that no man is to be discarded, every man is to be redeemed, and my life is the process whereby that redemption is brought about. And I do it by simply identifying the other with the ideal I want to externalize in my world… and you find yourself then not justifying but forgiving, and you will realize that freedom and forgiveness are indissolubly linked. You cannot be free and not forgive, for the one that you would bind and judge and condemn anchors you by your own judgment of him--for he is in you. And so by identifying him with the ideal you want to really realize you free yourself."

Forgiveness according to author Emmett Fox: "Setting others free means setting yourself free, because resentment is really a form of attachment. It is a Cosmic Truth that it takes two to make a prisoner; the prisoner--and a jailer. There is no such thing as being a prisoner on one's own account. Every prisoner must have a jailer, and the jailer is as much a prisoner as his charge. When you hold resentment against anyone, you are bound to that person by a cosmic link, a real, though mental chain. You are tied by a cosmic tie, to the thing that you hate. The one person perhaps in the whole world whom you most dislike is the very one to whom you are attaching yourself by a hook that is stronger than steel. Is this what you wish? Is this the condition in which you desire to go on living? Remember, you belong to the thing with which you are linked in thought, and at some time or other, if that tie endures, the object of your resentment will be drawn again into your life, perhaps to work further havoc. Do you think that you can afford this? Of course, no one can afford such a thing; and so the way is clear. You must cut all such ties, by a clear and spiritual act of forgiveness. You must lose him and let him go. By forgiveness you set yourself free; you save your soul. And because the law of love works alike for one and all, you help to save his soul too, making it just so much easier for him to become what he ought to be."

But how can we forgive when we have been so deeply injured that find it impossible; when we have tried and tried to forgive, but have found the task beyond us?

Many of us get stuck by thinking that forgiving someone means that we must keep them in our lives and work to change our experience with them. Forgiveness empowers us and does not keep us stuck in a cycle of abuse. It may only be possible to forgive once we have removed ourselves from the circumstances that require our forgiveness. We each are empowered the choice of who we take into our lives. Make those choices wisely, based on your ideals in life and in the people you love. Knowing that, "The people in my life treat me as I treat them, with respect and kindness," is your choice to make. Beyond that, your love can extend to all life by imagining the good in everyone, and love for everyone. Setting this tone brings harmony.

When we find that someone is continuously injuring us there are things we can do. First, we can see them in a differently light, as judgment can often bring conflict into our lives. When we judge someone as wrong or weird or controlling - we set the tone for conflict. Instead, we must see them in their highest potential, believe that we cannot be injured by anything they do or say, and allow them to blend into the background of our experience. If the conflict continues, we can ask ourselves, what part of me is this person expressing – who I am in the moment? What I judge in the moment? What has been lost, given or taken away? Which of the Essene Seven Mirrors of Relationship am I seeing? Conflict, when seen with this wisdom, can be a powerful tool for becoming.

Abuse is often enmeshed with the triad of victim, villain and hero. Transcending the mental state that allows these separate roles is recognizing that there are not victims, villains or heroes that are separate from one another. In an abuse scenario, they are interdependent, and each play their role so that the others can play also. By removing ourselves from any and all of these roles, we end the cycle of abuse.

Next, if the experience is injurious and not a matter of attitude or judgment, we can physically remove ourselves from the situation. End the relationship, change jobs, change homes – do what it takes to establish the distance needed so that you create an inner circle of people in your direct experience who treat you respectfully. Moving into this sovereignty in your awareness and in your life is a very big step in finding your harmony. By making this step, you are voicing, "I AM love."

Whatever action we take as we forgive, treating all people with love, not as separate, but in connection, is the key. This is what is meant by loving unconditionally.

To complete the process of true forgiveness, whatever our actions, we must be willing to let go of the memories that create anger and resentment. And we must be willing to hold all others in our heart with love. This is the process as the mystic Neville Goddard models it: "The art of forgiveness must be practiced daily, but first we must learn how to forgive. Repentance and faith are conditions of forgiveness, but true forgiveness is forgetfulness. Christianity and its doctrines make no sense to the worldly-wise, so why are people Christians? The promise that the dead will rise doesn't make sense to the mortal mind when the body is cremated and burned to ash; yet only by believing the story of redemption, can you truly forgive. You must learn to distinguish between the eternal human who occupies a state, and the state itself. This is the only means to forgiveness."

Neville goes on to teach us that everyone who fails us simply fails to live up to our ideal, and to find our harmony, instead of seeing the failure, see the potential in others: "If you will learn to distinguish between states of consciousness and their occupant, you can forgive everyone. How? By identifying the one you would forgive with the ideal he failed to realize. The highest ideal would be to identify him with the divine image itself."

It can be difficult for us to understand that forgiveness cannot happen when we are focused on the tangibles, on what we feel we have lost, on our injuries. No matter what has occurred in our experience, what happens is an invitation for greater self awareness. It is an invitation to understand that by bringing our awareness of the spirit in our experience into focus, we can forgive and create harmony. When Neville says, "Now, in this world, when you give something to someone else or sell it, you no longer possess it; but that is not true in the heavenly world. It is a world of sharing, where nothing is lost. In that world I can give you every faculty that has awakened within me and it becomes yours to use and give to another to use as they will," he is telling us that the "heavenly world" is the world of spirit, understood through our own imagination, felt in our hearts. It is here that the act of forgiveness is realized. Here, forgiveness sets a tone for our internal environment of peace and harmony.

"It's entirely up to you to practice the art of repentance, which is a radical change of feeling. A friend may have committed an act of violence and admitted his guilt. Practice the art of repentance by separating your friend (the actor) from the part he played, and identify him with the part you know in your heart that he would like to play," is what Neville tells us will establish harmony within us, and change our experience to one of love. The paradox here is that as we learn to live with unconditional forgiveness for ourselves and all others, we no longer experience the conflict that requires forgiveness.

REE WILL

**ALL POSSIBILITY EXISTS ALWAYS.
OUR FREE WILL ALLOWS OUR
AWARENESS OF POSSIBILITY WITH A
CHANGE IN VIEWPOINT**

I think the notion of free will is simple. God is the realm of infinite possibility. We choose possibility (free will) to create our individual experience. At some point in the journey, the two are integrated - the one and the many. Some people argue that free will is not the same as choice.

I think that all possibility is the realm of God, and we choose possibility, according to our viewpoint in the moment. Yet, if we are coexisting in an infinite number of possible realms, we are, in the same moment, living all different possibilities, each from a different viewpoint. As space time opens and all possibility is reached, each one limited viewpoint is simultaneously one in the all possibility. Everything you can imagine, you are. As you are experiencing yourself in separation from others, you are choosing, with   free will, which possibility to include in your viewpoint to shape your experience. You can change by choosing again. As long as you are separate and limited, the choice remains. There is a state of being where all possibility and all viewpoints are realized. Here, the choice is all of everything. This is the God within us.

In our lives, there is duality. But there is also more, there is non duality. And we can choose our viewpoint, giving us the feeling of free will. When we do, we are at the Pool of Bethesda (John 5:2) and our own self-image prevents our entry into the healing waters. Only our own higher ontology can stir the water for us, and in this awareness, we are the first into the water. Eventually, we can reach the point where we understand that what we are choosing is to be aware of our own divine nature in a different way. Our divine nature always is – it is our clear and ever present awareness – not our being but our awareness of being – "be still, and know that I AM God." (Psalm 46:10)

We cannot change what is, which is everything possible. But we choose our state of consciousness, our viewpoint, and in this, exercise our free will. By doing this, we change our experience of who we are and live our potentiality of all that is. This is how we, as some say, co create. We do so by making the possible real. We don't really change what is possible, we change our experience by changing our viewpoint, and that changes what is possible within our experience.

The process of becoming aware involves making choices and, breaking through old patterns. There is part of us that is infinite. This we know as God. There is part of us that is finite - this is our limited human experience. Together, they are the one and the many. The more we become in tune with the infinite, the more we are aware. The more our limitations are transcended, the more we are exempted of our limited human conditions. Patterns can be very limiting. Yet they provide that comfort zone and structure that allow us to feel safe and explore our consciousness and awareness until we are ready for the next steps. When we no longer need to take steps, we are in the flow. Thought patterns, behavior patterns - even our body has rhythmic patterns that can be changed to improve health.

Plato tells a story entitled "The Allegory of the Cave." He begins the story by describing a dark underground cave where a group of people are sitting in one long row with their backs to the cave's entrance. Chained to their chairs from an early age, all the humans can see is the distant cave wall in front of them. Their view of reality is solely based upon this limited view of the cave which but is a poor copy of the real world.

In addition to the chained people, there are other people in the cave. Plato refers to them as the puppet-handlers and they are the ones holding those in the cave captive. (It is important to realize that the prisoners do not realize this--in fact, the prisoners do not even realize that they are being held captive since this existence is all they have ever known.) Walking behind the prisoners, the puppet-handlers hold up various objects found in the real world. Due to a fire that is burning the mouth of the cave, the prisoners are able to see the objects and each other only as distorted, flickering shadows on the cavern wall in front of them.

Unfortunately, the prisoners cannot see the actual objects or the puppet-makers because they are unable to turn their heads. From childhood, "...their legs and necks [have been] in bonds so that they are fixed, seeing only [what is] in front of them.... As Plato goes on to later explain, "Truth would be literally nothing but the shadows of the images."

What Plato is saying, is that in our most basic human condition, we are the prisoners. The tangible world is our cave. The things that we perceive as real are actually just shadows on a wall. Just as the escaped prisoner ascends into the light of the sun, we amass knowledge and ascend into the light a greater reality, where ideas in our minds can help us understand the form of what is real.

When there is no separation, we are the people, and the shadow and the cave. We are the light and the source of the light. When self will is aligned with divine will, we move in grace but there is still separation. Yet, we may have a different viewpoint than the fellow in the cave - unless this is who we are in the moment and divine will is so. When we take on a separate viewpoint, we choose from infinite possibility, all that we are. Patterns serve a purpose here as in a kaleidoscope. They allow us structure, continuation and commonality. If we are not aware of them, they may dictate our actions. If we are conscious of them, and aware enough to understand that with our choices we create patterns of identity at will, and if we are aligned with divine will, these patterns reflect a grace in life and a harmony in experience. It is with choice that free will comes into play.

I believe that our role in regard to free will is to add possibility to the blossom of creation as it unfolds. We do this in how we hold our consciousness. We are the creation and the creators. We participate in the spiral, breathe life with love and beauty, or not. This is our choice.

We generate meaningful connections in our experience of consciousness, not the intellectual speculation of consciousness. States like cosmic consciousness (experience of all time and all others and all that is) can and are experienced in sleep and deep meditation or contemplation. Also, the undifferentiated, ineffable, omniscient, realm of all possibility can be experienced in sleep or deep meditation and contemplation. Once accessed, these states function in our awareness like background programs, running throughout our experience. Like this, they become a part of our complete experience. We all have the potentiality for this. We recognize and then experience when a change in viewpoint allows the possibility to manifest as real in our experience. Intellectual speculation may lead us to a change in viewpoint, or it may not. Our viewpoint manifests the experience. Our free will allows our choice.

GENEROSITY OF SPIRIT

UNCONDITIONALITY OF LOVE AND FORGIVENESS IS EXTENDED WITH GENEROSITY OF SPIRIT

Have you ever had a day when you felt completely in love with life, when you could see and *feel* spirit all around you, in everything and everyone? When you feel like this, you are generous of spirit.

Generosity of spirit can also be accomplished with thought. One of Neville Goddard's sayings is "Think of something wonderful for yourself and another." If our thoughts create our reality, then being generous in our thoughts will bring a generosity of spirit into our life that translates into peace and joy.

Giving our loved ones the space and love they need to work out their difficulties without agency or intervention can be generosity of spirit. Often, if we see someone struggling, we feel compelled to do something for them, fix things, or give our opinion or words of wisdom. Almost just as often, this makes things worse.

There are those times when we can be helpful. Usually if someone needs our help they will ask for it. It sometimes isn't easy to stand by and watch someone struggle. But sometimes – our generosity of spirit is all that is needed for others to feel loved and supported. Knowing that someone is in our lives that we can ask for help when necessary, who loves us enough to allow us to try and fail and try again – empowers us to continue to try.

If you can look out at everyone, and see them as becoming, remembering their highest potential and, in spite of their apparent mistakes and foibles, as doing the best they can in grace with their state of mind and stage of life - then you truly do have generosity of spirit.

"Whatsoever a man soweth, that shall he also reap." (Galatians VI) Your thoughts and deeds, good or bad, will repay you in kind. What you give, you get back. The thoughts and feelings that occupy your heart and mind will attract circumstances to your life of the same quality. They set a tone for your experience. This is life's way of reflecting back to us our own internal nature. This is our second chance, to understand our own ability to create our reality within our minds and hearts, and all around us.

At times, the world can be a big, unfriendly, cold place to live, full of darkness and shadow. Relating to others with respect and kindness is to be generous of spirit. Encouraging others around us to shine is a gift that we all can offer each other. In fact, when we extend this gift to others, we extend it to all of life. When we remember that it is more important to extend love than to be number one or front and center, we express our generosity of spirit.

G~OD~

WE ARE REALIZED BY BEING THE GOD WITHIN

Most of us feel that there is a source or creator or God or ultimate order to life. Connecting to this for some of us, is fleeting, takes effort and may even be something we think very little about. How do YOU connect with the spirit within you? How often do you connect? How does this connection effect your life?

Adolescence is the normal stage for us to begin to understand that we are not subject to programming by the external world. Until then, our families usually provide the protection necessary to safeguard us from any doom or suffering that may incur. Our childhood is the place to explore the world and begin to understand how our discoveries and choices effect our experience. This is a grand design, one that allows most of us time to find our own empowerment and begin to create lives that allow us harmony. Of course, if we were not fortunate enough to have been born to such design, whether by karma or bad luck, then we did not have the protection of a family, and felt the harshness of the external before we understood the workings of our own internal. Many folks like this are stuck in this emotional adolescence, blaming God and everyone else for all the bad that happens to them and all the evils of the world. Even under these circumstances, a change in viewpoint and an understanding that doom and suffering come to us through our own perception is possible though the hard work of self-examination or epiphany.

Do we have to have a God? I believe God is. God is within us all. Not all of us recognize or understand that it is this God within us that creates our experience according to our own filters of belief and viewpoint. Our experience is created whether we recognize this aspect of it or not. I believe that the quality of our experience improves with peace, harmony and love, if we do. Does this mean that folks who don't believe in God are doomed or suffer more or are wrong? No. It simply means that some of us believe in God and some don't. I believe that everyone is living to express who they are and moving into their potentiality that will be included in their expression. This is change. I can feel the harmony and completion of the entirety.

We all live a different experience. Our relationship to our experience creates it. This includes our relationship to ourselves, others, God, the earth etc. That is the many.

There is that part of life where we are all one. Some say this is the God within us or Christ consciousness. Paradoxically, the oneness doesn't negate our individuality, it empowers it.

A Vietnamese spiritual leader, Ching Hai, touches on this by answering the following:

Q: What is the first step one must take toward reaching God? A: We must pray that if God exists, please guide me, please help me. And stick to your religion and pray to that religious head that you believe in to help you. If you're Christian, pray to God, pray to Jesus, Santa Maria. If you're Buddhist, pray to Buddha, to Bodhisattvas, Quan Yin Bodhisattva, Amitabha Buddha, etc., to help you. That's the first step.

Gregg Braden teaches that prayer is the movement of our energy through our heart center. When we pray, we move our feeling up through our lower chakras, and our thoughts down through our higher chakras, through the heart chakra. Christ expressed this with his sacred heart teaching, as he showed us how to love and forgive unconditionally. Establishing our own sacred heart and moving our energy in this way create a constant prayer that connects us to God.

The second step, according to Ching Hai, is we must lead a virtuous life as prescribed in the Bible and in the Buddhist scriptures or in any other religious scriptures. I haven't seen any major religion which teaches people to do bad things. So follow your own religious ethic, as the second step.

As our lives become heart centered, our individual ethic will arise naturally. Rudolph Steiner tells us: "only that part of (man's) his conduct that springs from his intuitions can have ethical value in the true sense. And those moral instincts that he possesses through the inheritance of social instincts acquire ethical value through being taken up into his intuitions. It is from individual ethical intuitions and their acceptance by human communities that all moral activity of mankind originates. In other words, the moral life of mankind is the sum total of the products of the moral imagination of free human individuals." He is telling us that as we move in spirit, our individual ethic will arise naturally, from the inside out. We know intuitively that what we do to other, we also do to ourselves. And what we do to one, we do to all. Acting from our sacred heart with love, and listening to our intuitive ethical signals, allows us to develop our ethical individualism as we walk our path in spirit.

Ching Hai's third step is, we must find someone, and very importantly, who has known God, who has realized God, to show us something, to share with us the wealth that he or she has. For instance, if we want to speak English, what is the first step? Find a teacher -- one who can speak English (if you speak English.) If you find one who speaks Spanish (and you speak only English,) then no good. It's very easy.

Each on his own path will discover spirit, or God within. When we realize God within, our experience changes. The world around us becomes more loving. Why? Because love is the expression of God within us. And as we express this love, the world responds. If we follow the patterns of love in our life, look for love in the world around us in each moment, we are moving in spirit. When we are moving in spirit, it is reflected in the world around us - and the people around us. This is an essential discovery on the path to connecting with God.

To ask if God changes his plan, to me, is to ask if I have changed my relationship with God so as to effect a manifest change in my experience. God doesn't change; all possibility is all possibility, all inclusive. Through prayer, I change my viewpoint, or my relationship to God, and my experience changes because new possibility comes into my experience as a result of the change in me.

I think that what Jesus was saying is that the Christ potential is in everyman - which is why our faith can heal us (when we realize it). If you are thinking that any of his teachings are "a lie" then you are missing the essential truth of them, which is non dual, and this non duality is what leads us to the kingdom at hand. I questioned, for many years, how a man like Jesus could have possibly, actually, lived. Then I read the psychologist Carl Jung's *Memories, Dreams, Reflections* and fell in love with his idea that the collective unconscious of humanity allowed for the physical manifestation of the man Jesus. Humanity was ready for a savior. His life physically demonstrated to us the process of living life as close to God as possible, as did the life of Buddha and every savior and prophet on the planet. All of their teachings are diagrams for consciousness raising. Prophets are still all around us, we find them if we are in harmony with them, and we can hear them if we are listening. The message finds us when we are open to it. But we have to step out of our own stories and need for conflict and duality to truly understand the message.

I do not see God as separate from myself, or self separate from my experience. Therefore, someone or thing outside of myself is not effecting my experience completely external to me. I do understand that most folks understand God as objective, external to self and able to effect experience in ways that are separate from self. This is not what I believe.

I believe that God is an aspect of self that is: the ineffable, undifferentiated, all possibility, the uncreated (and created), omnipotent, omniscient and directly involved in a personal relationship with my individual self and all human beings. At this point, the point of God within, I am one with all life. The dynamic between my God and my individual self manifests my experience according to my viewpoint (beliefs.) One aspect of myself cannot be separated from the other, God, Christ (all humanity), me, my experience ... it all plays out in concert ... manifests through me into my experience. At the point that I and my experience are one, my experience is non dual.

Therefore, to me, prayer may just be "the language of God" or the Logos, as it moves between you and I. Logos connects, it moves, it manifests experience.

I still think that the Lord's Prayer is the perfect prayer, for different reasons now than I did as a child. Here is a quick synopsis of my latest interpretation. It includes setting my mind into the state of consciousness addressed in the prayer:

Our Father - the God state in me

Who art in heaven - the non dual state in me (where I and my experience are one)

Hallowed be thy name - the Logos in me (the meaning that passes between you and I)

Thy kingdom come - the viewpoint that allows heaven on earth

Thy will be done - action in grace that is of God within me

On earth as it is in heaven - all separation resolved within me

Give us this day - resurrecting self anew

Our daily bread - the Lord provides through the grace of manifestation

And forgive us our debts - become the self image in perfection, transcend karma

As we forgive those - live in recognition of the highest potential in everyone

Who have debt against us - the Christ consciousness, the union of humanity within us

And lead us not into temptation - live from the tree of life first

But deliver us from evil - Allow the fruit of the tree of knowledge to feel the life

Amen

My viewpoint is that nothing is external to God, and God is not external to me. God is an essential part of who I am. God is I AM in me. The paradox is that I am both differentiated (individual), and undifferentiated (God). I am God (Father), myself (Son), and my experience (Holy Spirit), expressed in states and stages and dimensions of consciousness.

I first accessed the state of God within me through meditation, then contemplation. Now, I believe it is part of the background program in my moment to moment consciousness. Ironically, I think that I most frequently fully access it during sleep, as it seems to become one of my primary sleep states. I know this because through vivid dreaming, I consciously recognize this state, and remember it as I awaken.

Someone once asked me "even if such a state (God) is perceivable what difference does it make?" It has made a difference to me in my viewpoint: how I understand the world and manifest experience; my character: how I respond to my experience; my relationships: how I treat others; my self-image: how I maintain my living self.

GUARDIANS OF THE THRESHOLD

OUR OWN FEARS GUARD THE THRESHOLD TO SPIRIT AND OUR ENTRY

I love Rudolph Steiner's story about the Guardians of the Threshold, who guard our entry into spiritual awareness, until we understand that one Guardian is the golden part of us who's beauty is too blinding and we must look away (or accept our self worth) and the other Guardian is our dark nature that holds the archetypes of the thief, whore, and all other undesirable natures that we look away from and cannot own up. Until we do, we cannot cross the threshold. Once we do, the guardians vanish, because they ARE us.

Some of us have the childish tendency of blaming someone or something outside of ourselves for our emotions. For instance, some of us blame religion for hatred and violence that we see in the world. The problems in our experience are only a reflection of what is within us that we each must own before we can cross the threshold. Organized religion may be limited in belief, but how will we know the limits unless we explore them? Religion does not hold prisoners; we ourselves with our beliefs do that.

There are also those who seek spirituality out of greed. They think that by knowing "the secret" of spirituality, they can get the material things that they want for themselves in life. These mysteries of life, once penetrated, purify. They do not deprave by meeting our personal agendas and self will. They do not take us farther into materialism and the world of our senses. The mystery always takes us further into spirit. If we seek spirituality with the agenda of possessing, we will be disappointed. If we explore the mystery in an effort to become and understand being, we will discover that "the Lord provides." But like Abraham on the mountain top, we must first be willing to let go of our earthly attachments, and realize our absolute reverence for the God within, before everything that we truly love comes back to us tenfold: "On the mountain of the LORD it will be provided." (Genesis 22:14)

I think it is worth noting, that according to the

Steiner teaching, once the threshold is crossed, the experience of the seeker changes to one who's experience does not contain direct violence and chaos - because duality is transcended, harmony can rule the day. It does not mean that duality no longer exists, only that it is no longer the experience of the seeker who has crossed the threshold.

You cannot cross the threshold into integration until you know that you can illuminate darkness yourself. The first Guardian contains all of our fears in aspects of good and evil. These fears prohibit our crossing the Threshold until we reconcile all good and evil within and see them interwoven into our whole being. The unseen then becomes seen.

The second Guardian, our golden shadow, is a sublime, luminous beauty impossible to describe. It holds our highest potential, and our low self image and our perceived limits keep us from embracing this Guardian and crossing the Threshold. To embrace the second Guardian we must realize that our highest possibilities (unseen) within ourselves creates our character and that our world of sense is a seed ground for the higher world. By embracing the second Guardian, everyone is redeemed and all are connected. We cannot cross the threshold in separation.

Once we can cross the threshold, according to Steiner, divine protection envelops us. Evil that was once part of our experience will no longer enter our direct experience. Because we have integrated evil and no longer hold it in separation, the greater is joined to the lesser and proceeds from us in love for all. We have thus been delivered from evil.

Our human existence at once subjects and exempts us from the ordinary conditions of sickness, ignorance, poverty and death. Our exemption is not ours until we fully understand that our objective states are unsuitable to the nature of our exemption. Our emotions and passions make us vulnerable to our more base instincts which subject us to ordinary conditions. Aspiring to faith will extort the emotions, both dark and golden, and allow our exemption. If we can transcend materialism and the world of our senses, integrate the good and evil, we are redeemed, reborn as whole, and what forms our experience is our purity of heart, expressed as love.

IMAGINATION

AWAKENED IMAGINATION IS OUR CREATIVE AWARENESS AND ACTIVE CONSCIOUSNESS

Our imagination is our biggest asset and tool for creating our lives and daily experience. If we limit our imagination, we limit our lives. Although our imaginations are unlimited, there are different stages of imagination, from the more mechanical memory and fantasy, to the more creative awakened imagination. All play an integral part in our lives, but the awakened imagination really holds the key to our quality of life. We use it when we are experiencing vivid dreaming or creative dreaming. It ramps up the quality and functionality of our dreams. We use it when we are in the witness, seeing ourselves doing, thinking, feeling and living. We use it when we are praying, unifying the one and the many within us. We use it when we move our subtle energies through our chakras in meditation. In other words, when we step out of our mechanical functions and move into our creative functions, we do so by using our awakened imagination.

When our world seems to fall apart and things start going wrong, what do we do? Do we blame ourselves or someone else? Do we start searching for causes and solutions? Do we hold on to our faith and believe that it will all work out?

The notion of the old dying and giving way for something new is as old as the ancient Hindu traditions, where Shiva is the destroyer of the world, following Brahma the creator and Vishnu the preserver, after which Brahma again creates the world and so on. Shiva is responsible for change both in the form of death and destruction and in the positive sense of the shedding of old habits.

Phenomenology tells us that in the deconstruction, every object shows itself as a set of possibilities, not merely as a determinate thing. To see a particular object is to see it in terms of possibilities. So while it seems that our experience is falling apart, possibility is also arising. If we can focus on the new possibility coming into our experience, instead of focusing on the old that no longer serves us and will fall away with change if we allow, we can see that all experience is experience of more - of possibility.

Neville Goddard believes that once we recognize the possibility, imagination is the key to creating our best possible lives. In his book, *Awakened Imagination,* he says: "The world presents different appearances accordingly, as our states of consciousness differ. What we see when we are identified with a state cannot be seen when we are no longer fused with it. By state is meant all that man believes and consents to as true. The world is a revelation of the states with which imagination is fused. It is the state *from* which we think that determines the objective world in which we live. If we detach ourselves from a state, and we may at any moment, the conditions and circumstances to which that union gave being vanish. The imaginative man does not deny the reality of the sensuous outer world of Becoming, but he knows that it is the inner world of continuous Imagination that is the force by which the sensuous outer world of Becoming is brought to pass."

This statement from Neville speaks more about our viewpoint than the event viewed or memory of it. We defuse from the event, according to Neville, when our viewpoint changes. Our viewpoint changes many times in our lives as we mature and evolve. As our viewpoint changes, so do our beliefs, perceptions, values, etc. My experience of life today is very different than it was when I was 5 years old because I view the world very differently. My intellectual, emotional, visceral and spiritual processing is different between the two ages because I identify differently with the information coming to me on these levels. This viewpoint defines the human maturation process. We progress in states and stages, each one resting on the foundation of the one before it, because we integrate them into our current viewpoint.

Where does that get us?

It gets us to where we are and where we can be. When we change our beliefs and that which we consent to be true, our experience changes because our internal state changes, and the process is inside out. Twenty years from now, I know that a memory of an event may not have the same emotional value to me as the original event, because my viewpoint will probably have changed, perhaps many times in the duration. The memory itself may even change with my change of belief and truth. Whether it brings me peace of mind or additional fear will depend on my internal state and my ability to use the tool of my awakened imagination.

I tend to agree with Neville, that finding my place of awakened imagination and envisioning, feeling and desiring circumstances that fit my highest potential and the greater good - will create this experience in my life. Will it change my life? Certainly, as this process, if it becomes my modus operandi, changes my responses, actions, relations, opportunities, possibilities and everything about me.

I reached a point in my life where I understood unity consciousness, meaning that I am connected to everything in life, and everything in my experience is of me. After this, I developed a greater awareness of my role in creating this experience, and what it reflects to me in each moment. Imagination is the key to this creative process. As feelings arise that tell me I am limited or separate from everything and everyone, I have learned to habitually evoke my awakened imagination to create feelings like joy or rapture. These feelings allow me to realize that I am part of the infinite wonders of creation and completely connected. If I find myself with negative thoughts about another, I can recognize them and then evoke my awakened imagination, to think of something wonderful for myself and another.

Using this tool of imagination to corral thoughts and feelings allows me to create an internal environment according to my highest potential by maintaining a resonance of creative good, thus bringing what is good into my experience.

Exercising my awakened imagination has become a daily routine for me. I think that the most efficacious times are right before sleep and upon waking. Before sleep, if I can imagine the qualities and experiences that I desire in my life with awakened imagination, the quality of my sleep and dreaming is dramatically improved. I engage more in vivid and creative dreaming and feel better rested during the day. I truly believe that in this way, what I imagine my life to be, will become my experience.

In that twilight period where I am coming back into consciousness, coming out of a dream or slowly becoming awake, I step into the witness and recognize what is coming into my awareness, using awakened imagination to turn it all into what I desire my life to be, adding my highest potential to all thoughts and memories. I try to make sure that before I get up, I feel integrated and reconciled, and that my primary feeling is joy or love. In this way, I can begin my day expressing love for myself and all creation.

Neville Goddard tells us, "Every moment of time you are imagining what you are conscious of, and if you do not forget what you are imagining and it comes to pass, you have found the creative cause of your world." With our awakened imagination, we create the fabric of our lives.

Resistance

THE LESSONS OF RESISTANCE RECONCILLE OPPOSITION AND GUIDE US FROM DUALITY TO NON DUALITY

Resistance itself is a tool for learning. At the age of two, we learn the wonderful power of NO, and continue to use it until sometime as an adult we learn, that there isn't no, there is only yes. Because even when we use the word no, we are consenting to something – either feeding our ego by insisting that things go our way, or allowing our experience to flow with grace by offering "no" to others as a learning tool. When we know the difference, we know that there is no other. And no becomes yes.

Resistance itself is a measure of opposition, and there are enormous lessons to be learned and skills to acquire in reconciling opposites. Indeed, many of the sacred teachings see the soul as having a function of reconciling opposites in fulfilling karma, repenting sin or mastering kundalini. On the conscious level, problem solving, conflict resolution and negotiating are all basic skills that are learned from childhood to adulthood. They define our resilience and efficacy, and require mastery of resistance. It is in the reconciliation of opposites as, often through paradox, as in the practice of Tao ("The cause and the effects are aspects of the same, one thing. They are both mysterious and profound. At their most mysterious and profound point lies the "Gate of the Great Truth.") The practice of Tao requires that we can finally let go of our need for resistance and move in unity.

In the Hindu scripture, Bhagavad-Gita, Sri Krishna calls Arjuna a hypocrite and a coward because of his refusal to fight. This is a great lesson for us all to learn, that in all matters the two extremes are alike. The extreme positive and the extreme negative are always similar (actually complimentary.)

The story tells us that one man does not resist because he is weak, lazy, and cannot, not because he will not; the other man knows that he can strike a fatal blow if he likes; yet he not only does not strike, but blesses his enemies. The one who from weakness resists not, commits a sin, and as such cannot receive any benefit from the non-resistance; while the other would commit a sin by offering resistance.

When the vibrations of light are too slow, we do not see them, nor do we see them when they are too rapid. So with sound; when very low in pitch, we do not hear it; when very high, we do not hear it either. The difference between resistance and non-resistance is much the same.

It is a big awareness leap for those that must resist: from learning the nature of resistance by resisting, to being able to resist, but refraining out of compassion. In the moment, what comes up will tell us how to respond according to our own view. If it includes aggressive resistance so that we can learn the nature of resistance, then the outcome will be to everyone's benefit.

In words of the Hindu sage Vivekananda, two ways are left open to us--the way of the ignorant, who think that there is only one way to truth and that all the rest are wrong, and the way of the wise, who admit that, according to our mental constitution or the different planes of existence in which we are, duty and morality may vary. The important thing is to know that there are gradations of duty and of morality--that the duty of one state of life, in one set of circumstances, will not and cannot be that of another.

Until we learn the nature of resistance, refusing to fight will only bring the event back into our life again and again until we learn. And, each time we are called to resist, we may find our sense of our duty and morality different than ever before. These evolve with application, until they become intrinsic and flow naturally from our highest nature.

Once we know and fully own that we can prevail in any circumstance, knowing that we can deal the fatal blow but choose not to, provides the outcome that benefits everyone. After we reach that point, violence falls out of our direct experience because we have learned what we need to from it. If we are living in a state of mind that is peaceful, does not judge, allows each their own view, and can hear and see spirit in all of experience - our direct experience will reflect peace, not violence to us. Each step of the process is formed by who we are in the moment.

SHADOW

GOLDEN AND DARK SHADOW REFLECTED IN OTHERS, WAIT WITHIN US, FOR OUR FREEDOM

All of us at some time in our lives are confronted with parts of ourselves that get in our way, that limit us, and keep us realizing all that we are. It might be a manipulative behavior, or avoidance. It might be an unexplainable attraction to bad boys, or even attraction to a "golden child" or person who seems to move in complete grace. This is our shadow in action, and our ego instinctively looks away because shadow holds the limited portions of our personality and habits developed in the past that no longer serve, and are not part of conscious awareness. These are the parts of ourselves that we have learned to repress.

Our dark shadow holds repressed negativity while our golden shadow holds our repressed potentiality. These two aspects of shadow are the Guardians of the Threshold to spirit, to non duality, and to living in grace. They prevent us from being all we can be, from reaching our highest potential, and from living our lives in the experience of heavenly, loving spirit.

The shadow can be comprised of portions of our collective psyche. This comes up as circumstances or emotions that separate us as a group. It can also present as external fascination or spectacle that holds our attention, and thus keeps us from accessing internal resources and connecting with the group in spirit.

We usually project our shadow into places where it is "safe" to show this side of us, like our closest relationships. We instinctively know that the people we love the most give us the best chance to transform our shadow aspect by recognizing it, and then initiating and sustaining expanded awareness. This transformation process removes limitation and allows us to release what no longer serves, having recognized that it does not fit the "big picture" of integration and unity.

In order to understand repetitive patterns in relationships, Dr. Carl Jung suggested what we understand the psychological rule: "The psychological rule says that when an inner situation is not made conscious, it happens outside as fate. That is to say, when the individual remains undivided and does not become conscious of his inner opposite, the world must perforce act out the conflict and be torn into opposing halves."

This acting out involves projecting our shadow aspects, or our belief in our own limitations. The more we know about ourselves, the more choices we have, and our limitations fall away. We can then choose not to behave in a certain way. When we don't understand our behavior, it will take on a compulsive, autonomous element. Projection is an unconscious psychological mechanism. We all project onto other people parts of ourselves that we disown, that we deny. We will usually not identify with the projected quality or characteristic at all. We perceive the projection as them, not us. Until we understand and accept our own shadow.

One of Dr. Carl Jung's real contributions, was to point out that our shadow, or the rejected aspects of ourselves or undeveloped potential, contains all sorts of creative, positive content. If you were a musically gifted child, for instance, and you dreamed about playing guitar or composing a symphony but your parents felt that they wanted you to perform academically and go to law school and join the family law firm, your musical ability was repressed into shadow to please your parents. This is your golden shadow, your repressed potentiality, limited only by the fact that it is unrecognized and unaccepted.

To disown or look away from your shadow is to guarantee its return in one form or another. Your shadow is all you. Accepting all aspects of who you are makes for a much less stressful life. Now the trickier part - accepting those parts of your experience that are also you, cast into others and into relationship as your shadow for recognition and acceptance, the parts that you have not yet considered. This consideration is often met with much resistance by folks accustomed to crying "it's them not me." An understanding friend or loved one can sometimes help us see these "holes" that we haven't seen yet in ourselves. Most of us have shadow because as long as we are alive we will be self in evolution. A graceful shadow process can give us more harmony.

I think, in some strange way, the shadow is our friend. We are incarnate beings in a relative world, and shadow is inevitable. Once we recognize its presence, we can create ways to deal with it that moves us into higher states of consciousness. What we create casts its own shadow, and the process begins anew. Maybe shadow is the space between the rungs on the ladder of progress!

During my own shadow dance, golden shadow has been just as difficult to integrate as dark shadow. We are taught from an early age to believe in our limits. No wonder, when it comes time to embrace the infinite within us, we find the dance step challenging.

The spectrum of humanity does indeed exist, and allows for evolution within a lifetime as well as the accomplishments of humanity as a whole. It is a wonderful thing that we can eat a cup of yogurt without having to buy the cow, milk it, make the yogurt etc. We certainly stand on the shoulders of all that went before us and benefit (or not) from the works of all others around us. Shadow presents itself to us in the array of this experience when we find something occurring again and again, and we have a big emotional charge about it - good or bad. This is our clue that shadow is at work.

I think the key notion here is "repetitive." One dumb ass mooching neighbor bothering you does not mean this trait is part of your shadow. If you find yourself in relationships over and over again with dumb ass moochers and this gives you a big emotional charge, then it might be something worth looking at in yourself. And I don't think that it always means that it is something that you are but deny. Shadow may exist because the quality is something you judge in a very big way, and you project shadow again and again as a challenge to let go of your judgmental self. Sometimes we don't let go because we get something out of seeing others as "wrong." It also establishes our separateness from our dumb ass neighbor, and establishes rational limits to our neighborly feelings. Sometimes these serve us, providing us safe harbor from what we see as wrong with the world, and allowing us a feeling of superiority. We experience this over and over until we can let those feelings go, and realize that the weaknesses we see in others are really projections of our own limitations.

On the other side of the coin, there is certainly nothing wrong with feeling harmony in a group. But if you feel yourself extremely attracted to folks that have a particular wonderful quality, over and over again - then it may be worth asking yourself, is there something that all these folks have in common that I might be denying in myself? When we don't ask ourselves this, it again establishes limits to what we can become, because heck - we could never be THAT wonderful.

The contemporary philosopher Ken Wilber gives us a process for integrating our shadow in his 3-2-

1 *Process*, that instructs us to: first choose a significant experience in your life that gives you a strong emotional charge, either positive or negative. Then: (3) *face it* by describing what upsets you or attracts you about the experience; (2) *talk to it* in an imaginary dialogue, addressing what bothers you and speaking the conversation aloud. Try using 1st, 2nd or 3rd person whatever feels most comfortable but be sure to end in the 1st person; and (1) *be it* by taking on the qualities that either annoy or fascinate you, beginning to embody the traits described in your conversation. To complete the process, recognize these traits that were previously disowned in yourself and experience the part of you that is this trait. Own and integrate this trait into yourself. We can only let go of something we have first owned. For this reason, recognition of our shadow allows us passage into those parts of ourselves that require release of identity.

"Remaining like a child is the most valuable trait a person can have." The marvelous viewpoint of St. Therese tells us that loving like children gives us a purity of experience. She instructs us: "in love we all live and move and have our being," and by abandoning all other care and focusing on this, we retain the innocence that is childlike that allows us all that is sacred in life. I think we all yearn to return to that part of us that as a child was unjaded by the world worries. Achieving this is monumental, and much to be admired. While St. Therese certainly had her shadow, I do believe that this viewpoint always reconciled it for her.

"When I was a child, I spoke like a child, thought like a child, and reasoned like a child. When I became a man, I gave up my childish ways. Now we see only an indistinct image in a mirror, but then we will be face to face. Now what I know is incomplete, but then I will know fully, even as I have been fully known." (Corinthians 13) I think this passage from Paul tells us that we are born with this wonderful quality that is outside of ego, and can return to it once we are fully known. This requires a full maturation and transcendence of ego, and a step across that shadowy threshold and into spirit.

For those of us who have experienced a broken heart, there is great vulnerability in this shadow dance. It is natural to pull in emotionally after heartbreak, and give ourselves the safe space to heal. Someone told me that a broken heart is an open heart. I think eventually, once we get our bearings back, our hearts can open in new ways, once they are ready to open again. We must be who we are…brilliant. There may be folks who need to criticize or oppose, but just smile and hold a space for them to become more than that. If we can hold them in compassion, and not allow them to diminish or hurt our feelings, they WILL become more than that, and so will we, by embracing them as our own shadow. Those vulnerabilities of ours are shadow that when projected, tell us that we are separate and less than worthy. It isn't true, that is just the wound coming back, asking to be healed. If we can remember ourselves as beautiful, connected, powerful, intelligent, insightful, creative, loving – we will experience our wounds and those conflicts differently – with confidence and compassion for ourselves and all others involved. Then, without missing a beat, we will move the circumstance into a positive outcome that serves everyone's highest potential.

When we come to the same place with our science and our mysticism, the importance of understanding our viewpoint and our place in it cannot be denied. That threshold of fear, where our own shadow keeps us from the non dual experience, is where I find most verbose folks whose need to rail against the world's ills might be threatened by taking responsibility for the world in a new morality. This anxiety can be difficult to let go of, like the fear that guards the threshold. Letting go of the need to find the world wrong so that we can feel right is releasing our own golden shadow. What we cannot know without crossing the threshold, is that releasing the shadow is also stepping into it, and opening the door to infinite possibility for ourselves and our experience. We choose possibility with our viewpoint, creating our experience, and when we cross the threshold and accept the will of God as infinite possibility, we accept all that is as our own. The paradox can be unimaginable, especially to those who hold tight to fear, good and evil and its sweet fruit, me and not me. The promise of the Kingdom and infinite possibility is just beyond, and so much more...

Bibliography

Thomas Troward, *Bible Mystery and Bible Meaning,* New York, NY: Dodd Mead & Co. Publishers 1913

Stephen Mitchell, *Tao Te Ching,* New York, NY: Harper and Row Publishers, 1988

Steven Mitchell, *Bhagavad Gita: A New Translation,* New York, NY: Three Rivers Press, Publisher 2000

Rudolph Steiner, *The Way of Initiation and Its Results;* First Americanized Edition. Ferndale, MI: Trismegistus Press 1980

Rudolph Steiner, *The Philosophy of Freedom,* Forest Row, East Sussex: Rudolph Steiner Press, Publisher, 1964

Neville Goddard, Lecture: True Forgiveness; 04-01-1969

Neville Goddard, *Awakened Imagination,* Marina Del Ray, CA: DeVorss & Co., Publisher, 1954

Martin Heidegger, Ted Sadler, *The Essence of Truth: on Plato's Cave Allegory and Theaetetus,* Bongay, Suffolk: MPG Books, Ltd., Publisher 2002

Bibliography (cont.)

Ken Wilber, *Integral Spirituality*; Boston, MA: Shambhala Publications, Inc. 2006

Gregg Braden, *Secrets of the Lost Mode of Prayer*, Carlsbad, CA: Hay House, Inc., Publisher, 2006

Gregg Braden, *Walking Between the Worlds: The Science of Compassion*, Questa, New Mexico, Sacred Spaces Ancient Wisdom, Publisher, 1996

Emmet Fox, *The Sermon on the Mount, The Key to Success in Life*, New York, NY: Harper Collins Publishers 1989

Ching Hai Wu Shang Shih, *The Key of Immediate Enlightenment*, Sedona, AZ: Infinite Light Publishing Company, 1993

Carl Gustav Jung, *Memories, Dreams, Reflections*, New York, NY: Random House, Publisher 1965

Barbara Hannah, *Jung His Life and Work*, New York, NY: GP Putnam's Sons, 1976

Alfred Kazin, *The Portable Blake*, New York, NY: Viking Press, Publisher 1946

www.ingramcontent.com/pod-product-compliance
Lightning Source LLC
Chambersburg PA
CBHW031548080326
40690CB00054B/744